RHODE ISLAND
A Picture Book to Remember Her by

CRESCENT BOOKS
NEW YORK

CLB 1750
©1987 Illustrations and text: Colour Library Books Ltd.,
  Guildford, Surrey, England.
Printed and bound in Barcelona, Spain by Cronion, S.A.
All rights reserved.
1987 edition published by Crescent Books, distributed by Crown Publishers, Inc.
ISBN 0 517 62596 2
h g f e d c b a

There are so many farms and forests, wetlands and bays in Rhode Island, it's hard to believe that it is the smallest of the 50 states. Though it is only 48 miles from the northern to the southern tip, it has 76 miles of Atlantic Ocean shoreline and 170 miles of coastline on its inland waters. Narragansett Bay, extending from Newport to Providence, is bordered by hills and pastureland and dotted with small, peacefull towns. The overall effect is that there is plenty of room to spread out in Rhode Island.

It all began in 1636, when a clergyman named Roger Williams had a falling out with the Massachusetts Puritans and moved down to the head of Narragansett Bay to found a more liberal colony at Providence. Within ten years others had followed him and there were thriving towns at Newport, Warwick and Portsmouth, too. They eventually banded together and Williams secured a royal charter to make it all legal. The city of Newport had been settled by John Clarke and William Coddington, who had been banished from Massachusetts for their liberal tendencies regarding religion. They bought an island in the Bay that the Indians who sold it to them had called Aquidneck. Before long they changed its name to the "Isle of Rhodes," which later became the basis for the name of the whole state. The suggestion had come as far back as 1524, when the explorer Verrazano landed on Block Island and noted in his log that it reminded him of the Mediterranean island of Rhodes.

The lure of true religious freedom brought hundreds to the new colony, and Rhode Island quickly shifted from farming to shipbuilding and seafaring. In the years before the Revolutionary War, Newport was the center of the slave trade and in the process became one of the wealthiest cities in America. In spite of it, the state outlawed slaves in 1774, almost 35 years before the rest of the country followed suit.

Privateers took up the slack and made Newport wealthier still, and by the 1760s it was the resort of choice for plantation owners from the South and from the West Indies who went north to escape the heat of the summer. Even though the city went into a decline as a major port after the Revolution, the tourist wave continued and after the Civil War, Ward McAllister, a former Southerner who had known Newport as youngster, set himself up as the organizer of New York society and lured the likes of the Astors and Bellmonts to the city at the end of Narragansett Bay.

The houses they built to demonstrate their wealth are what lure the tourists there today, but the real lure is what it has always been: a unique combination of wild seascapes and peaceful landscapes.

Facing page: Pawcatuck Seventh Day Baptist Church at Westerly.

Top: boats at anchor in the harbor at Watch Hill, a popular vacation resort on Little Narragansett Bay. Among the town's attractions is the famous Flying Horse Carousel (above) of 1883, as well as the statue that adorns the Ridley Watts memorial (left). To the east of the town lies romantically-named Misquamicut, with its fine surrounding beaches (facing page and overleaf).

The waters of Rhode Island have long been famed for their fine fishing, and towns such as Narragansett (above and top) continue to rely on the sea for their livelihood. Local trawler and fishing fleets (facing page) maintain the town's claim as the "world tuna capital." Left: the octagonal Point Judith Lighthouse, near the small fishing village of Galilee.

Among Newport's many historic landmarks are the weatherboarded Trinity Church (facing page) and the Old Colony House (top, left of center), both designed by Richard Munday. It was in the elegant brick building on Washington Square that Rhode Island declared its independence from Great Britain in 1776. Equally famous, but almost 200 years its junior, is Newport Bridge (previous pages, above and right).

Sailing is a sport that generates almost religious fervor in Newport (these and previous pages), and the city is known worldwide as a major boating center. Sleek, tall-masted sailing craft, luxurious motor cruisers and small pleasure boats fill the waters off Newport throughout the year, but especially during the various races, regattas and boat shows that the city hosts. As well as being a mecca for the boating enthusiast, Newport has long been famous as a Navy town – it was, until 1973, home of the Atlantic Fleet and still houses the Naval Education and Training Center and the Naval War College.

Quaint, cobbled Thames Street (right and facing page, top) lined with shingled and weatherboarded shops, is one of Newport's harbor-area tourist haunts. Trinity Church (above) stands at the intersection of Spring and Church Street, while Bellevue Avenue (top and facing page bottom) is famous for the palatial mansions that line its southern reaches.

Previous pages: the sleek arc of the Newport Bridge spans the waters of the bay, linking the city with Jamestown, on Conanicut Island, to the west. Newport's incredible mansions recall a period in the city's history when the rich and famous built their summer "cottages" here. Today, these buildings are maintained by the Preservation Society of Newport County and are open to the public. Marble House (top), with its magnificent dining room (facing page bottom left) and ballroom (facing page bottom right), built in 1892 for William K. Vanderbilt, is among the most luxurious of these cottages, while Cornelius Vanderbilt's The Breakers (above and facing page top) has the distinction of being the largest.

Distinctly French in character, Rosecliff (top and facing page) was modelled on the Grand Trianon at Versailles for Mrs. Hermann Oelrichs, and features a huge ballroom (facing page top) that witnessed some of the most dazzling social gatherings of the early 20th century. Credit for the establishment of Newport as a high-society resort, however, is often given to Caroline Astor, the doyenne of American high society at the turn of the century, whose sumptuous Beechwood home (above) was bought for her by her husband in 1890. The house was designed by Calvert Vaux, the English architect involved in the planning of New York's Central Park.

Eisenhower Park (left and top), bordered by Washington Square, is overlooked by historic Old Colony House (facing page). One-time seat of the state's government, it is in this building that George Washington is said to have planned the battle of Yorktown. At the other end of the square is the Brick Market with its gift shops and cafes (above). Overleaf: Newport waterfront.

Ornate wrought ironwork, sweeping marble
staircases, columns and pilasters grace the grand
entrance hall and gallery (above, top and facing page
bottom) of the Elms (these pages), built for the coal
magnate Edward J. Berwind. Overleaf: Chateau-sur-
Mer, with its ornate Victorian interior.

Right: a Newport sailboard maker gives a modern-day interpretation to Rhode Island's fine tradition of sailing craft construction. Above: the massive spars of Newport Bridge create a sleek, flowing shape when viewed at a distance (facing page bottom). Top: an aerial view of the grand homes dotted over Brenton Point. Facing page top: Brenton Cove.

Previous page: a view of Newport from the east. These pages: hundreds of miles of shoreline, and good Atlantic breezes, make Rhode Island one of the nation's leading yachting centers. Newport itself is a world-renowned sailing center, for long best-known as the venue for the America's Cup races. The Newport to Bermuda race is another high point in the international racing calendar. Overleaf: silhouettes of Newport at dusk.

Polished wood and a forest of masts and rigging, as well as mementoes of former sailing days (left), lend an air of timelessness to the waterfront at Bowen's Wharf (these pages). This cobbled dockside area, with its craft shops and restaurants, is a popular Newport development.

Brick arches topped by white stucco pilasters grace the solid exterior of the grand old Brick Market (facing page bottom) of 1762. At the hub of the city's trade in the 18th century, when Newport was one of New England's major commercial centers, the building also served as the City Hall from 1853-1900. Today, this historic landmark serves as a gift shop and art gallery. On the fringes of the city the attractions are somewhat different, yet no less appealing. Beautiful coastal scenery can be experienced along the Cliff Walk, a three-mile route that passes some of the magnificent mansions and ends at Bailey's Beach (top). Further west, near Brenton Point, rocky outcrops enclose the rippled waters of Greens Pond (facing page top). Above: a view of the city from King Park.

For aficionados (right), Newport sailing regattas (top, facing page top left and overleaf) are a fascinating and exciting time, while for the uninitiated they offer an opportunity to enjoy a picnic with friends (above). To the fisherman (facing page top right), however, the city's waters offer far more attractive possibilities.

Designed by the noted New York partnership of McKim, Mead and White, the shingled buildings of Newport Casino (these pages), along Bellevue Avenue, served as an exclusive country club for the area's rich and famous inhabitants. From 1881-1914, before moving to their present home at Forest Hills, the L.T.A. championships were played on the Casino's tennis courts. Today, the buildings house the International Tennis Hall of Fame and Museum, while the courts are still used for tennis tournaments during July and August.

Whatever the event, be it a classic 12 meter-event or a modest dinghy race, there is never a shortage of competitors or spectators during sailing regattas. Vantage points abound along the Newport shoreline, where a pleasant day can be spent watching the proceedings. Newport Bridge (facing page and overleaf) provides an ever-present backdrop to the proceedings.

Previous pages: Newport Beach (main picture) and environs. At the head of Narragansett Bay lies the city of Providence (these pages), sole capital of Rhode Island since 1900. As befits an important commercial center, the city's downtown area (facing page) boasts a wealth of modern architecture, while older structures, such as the State House (top), the Round Top Congregational Church (left) and those on Thomas Street (above), are lovingly preserved.

Previous pages: the elegant interior of Providence's Arcade shopping center. These pages: the grounds and buildings of Brown University, in the College Hill area of Providence. Founded in 1764 at Warren, the college was later moved to its present location and is now among the nation's foremost seats of learning. Overleaf: Kennedy Plaza.